Minimalism

Efficient Home Decor Strategies For Tackling Clutter And Simplifying Your Living Space

(The Indispensable Manual For Streamlining Your Household And Everyday Routine)

Laszlo Schlögl

TABLE OF CONTENT

What Is Minimalism? 1

Simplify Your Mindset, Residence, And Existence 10

How to Teach Your Children That Less Is More 15

An Ideal Moment For Reorganizing Your Life: Purge Your Thoughts And Invigorate Your Spirit.. 39

The Many Benefits Of Practising Less 63

Social Advantages.. 78

Examination Of Minimalism In Comparison To Consumerism 88

Define Yourself 121

The Value Of Clearing Mental Clutter To Improve Your Life 134

What Is Minimalism?

There does not exist a prescribed set of principles or a universally accepted criterion that delineates the concept of minimalism. In a manner akin to leading a modest lifestyle, minimalism is a notion that can encompass various interpretations among individuals. If you possess an inclination to explore and gain knowledge about minimalism, it becomes crucial to develop a comprehensive understanding of minimalism in accordance with your personal perspective.

What is minimalism?

According to renowned minimalist Nicholas Burroughs,

Minimalism can be defined as achieving the ideal balance or appropriate quantity of something, rather than being characterized by any deficiency or absence.

Minimalism encompasses more than mere possession of material items. Minimalism entails prioritizing and dedicating oneself to the essentials, as opposed to expending time, effort, and resources on particulars. According to the esteemed minimalist Joshua Becker, minimalism involves actively prioritizing the things that hold the most value to us, while simultaneously removing any unnecessary elements that divert our attention from them.

The definition provided above elucidates and elucidates the concept of minimalism for a majority of individuals. Minimalism is centered around developing a distinct and profound understanding of one's core values and their significance in life. Focusing solely on the foremost thoughts, activities, efforts, and possessions, while intentionally eliminating any extraneous elements that hinder the pursuit of one's cherished priorities and possessions. Each individual possesses a unique perception of what constitutes minimalism. Each individual possesses a distinct and personal set of values.

Minimalism entails developing the ability to concentrate.

What are the utmost significant and invaluable entities in your life? By directing your attention towards the crucial and esteemed aspects of existence, you will come to recognize that while possessions may be abundant, only a select few truly contribute genuine worth to your life. Similar to being knowledgeable about where it is unwise to allocate investments, minimalism entails the discernment of what possessions and elements are unnecessary in one's life. Subsequently, proceed with its removal and remain at ease with the adjustment.

Minimalism is an ongoing practice.

Achieving a state of minimalism is not attainable. It pertains to the consistent pursuit of self-improvement through ongoing personal challenges. It poses a challenging task to discern and eliminate superfluous possessions, retaining solely those that hold genuine significance in one's life. Minimalism entails the constant evaluation and reassessment of one's priorities on a day-to-day basis.

Minimalism involves the concept of time.

Simplification of one's life can be achieved through the directed attention towards the fundamental aspects. This affords individuals liberation from erroneous beliefs, apprehensions, culpability, and anxieties. By prioritizing only the essential aspects of life, you provide yourself with an increased capacity to experience a sense of freedom and ease. You develop a heightened level of adaptability and consequently maximize your time efficiency. Minimalism enables individuals to direct their attention towards their invaluable asset - time.

What minimalism is not

There exist numerous misconceptions surrounding the concept of minimalism. The following is a compilation of a few examples:

Minimalism entails relinquishing possession of all personal belongings. Minimalism does not entail relinquishing all of one's possessions.

Your primary objective should revolve around the benefits derived from eliminating elements that do not contribute value to your life.

Minimalism presents challenges: Minimalism does not pose hardships to your life. On the contrary, the inverse holds true, whereby embracing a minimalist lifestyle leads to the simplification of one's life.

Frugality and minimalism are synonymous: Minimalism encompasses more than mere financial savings, and both concepts are distinct from one another.

The notion that minimalism exclusively applies to young and unattached individuals is likewise unsubstantiated.

Minimalism is not exclusively confined to material possessions: While purging excess belongings is imperative, minimalism encompasses more than just the physical realm.

Alcohol

Alcohol consumption may be inconsequential for individuals who demonstrate the ability to drink moderately, whereas for others, it may manifest as a severe addictive behavior. Alcohol can ruin lives. Alcohol does not act as a black hole for all individuals, nevertheless, it should not be disregarded that it may eventually assume a black hole-like status. If you consume a moderate amount of alcohol occasionally, it is unlikely that you are at risk of becoming excessively dependent. However, if you find yourself compelled to consume a consistent amount of alcohol each night following work, as well as an increasing quantity on weekends, it is possible that you are approaching a perilous situation.

Alcoholism presents a significant health concern, encompassing both physical and mental well-being. Ethanol is fundamentally a mild toxic substance, and the intoxication sensation experienced is a result of the gradual circulation of the toxin within our body. Consistently subjecting our bodies to toxins over an extended duration can lead to significant health complications, such as liver cirrhosis and a heightened susceptibility to specific forms of cancer. Even within a limited timeframe, it presents a hazard—excessive intake of alcohol in brief intervals has the potential to result in fatality. Abstaining from alcohol abruptly can potentially lead to a fatal outcome.

For individuals who engage in excessive alcohol consumption, a single evening spent socializing at a bar with companions has the potential to exhaust their entire week's wages. Drinks aren't cheap. Consuming only a limited number of beverages within a span of one or two hours can swiftly incur costs exceeding $50. While not everyone succumbs to the vortex of alcohol, the potential for such a descent is significant. Despite its widespread consumption and legal status in many jurisdictions, alcohol is considered a substance with drug-like properties, and therefore, it is advisable to exercise moderation when consuming it.

Simplify Your Mindset, Residence, And Existence

Simplifying your life and imbuing it with purpose, significance, and organization hinges upon the act of decluttering. Comprehend that true worth does not derive from an abundance of possessions, but rather from those that hold significance. In the upcoming span of 4 days, you will be implementing this principle across various facets of your life, with the aim of decluttering and organizing them to the greatest extent feasible.

Day 4: Systematize and Arrange Your Residence, Focusing on One Room at a Time

A minimalist dwelling epitomizes the essence of prioritization, accommodating a reduced number of indispensable elements. Even when you make additional purchases for your household, you acquire items that hold personal significance. In order to establish an appealing environment within your residence, it is advisable to allocate the fourth day for the purpose of decluttering. Today, select a specific room within your residence that exhibits high levels of disarray and lack of organization, and initiate the process of decluttering said space.

Although it is possible to declutter and organize the entire house within a single day, engaging in such an undertaking may lead to feelings of extreme fatigue and overwhelm. These emotions could potentially diminish your motivation to adhere to your minimalism objectives and even prompt you to abandon your goal. In order to prevent this from occurring and to ensure that you derive satisfaction from the entire journey toward embracing a genuine minimalist lifestyle, please bear in mind that consistent progress and a deliberate pace yield favourable outcomes.

Upon selecting a designated area for decluttering, carefully examine the space and select one to five items that are incompatible with the room or fail to contribute any meaningful value to its purpose. Items that are in poor condition, no longer serve a purpose, hold no intrinsic value, or are present in excess may be removed from that particular enclosure. When organizing your bathroom, as an example, if you find yourself with three soaps occupying the soap dish when only one is necessary, it would be advisable to eliminate the surplus two. If there happen to be vacant shampoo bottles resting on the shelf, please dispose of them as well.

After having eliminated any unnecessary items from your space, proceed to thoroughly clean it, and subsequently arrange the belongings you choose to retain in an orderly manner, ensuring that each item is assigned a designated spot. The area will immediately exhibit a greater sense of spaciousness, organization, and overall pleasantness to your perception. When disposing of any object, it is important to be mindful of your thoughts. If you notice that you are entertaining notions of acquiring a replacement or additional item, it is advisable to deal with such thoughts in a constructive manner.

Henceforth, establish a routine of regularly purging a section of your home or a specific room on a weekly basis. It is versatile enough to serve as either a clothing storage space, a compartment, or even an entire chamber. By following this approach, you will eliminate superfluous items and enhance the overall quality of your life.

Day 5: Eliminate Superfluous Activities

In a similar vein to how you organized and simplified your living space, it is now necessary for you to streamline your daily schedule and remove any superfluous engagements or pursuits you may have taken on.

Consider your fundamental principles and aspirations for your future, and assess the endeavors you elect to partake in and those you wish to sustain your involvement in. As an illustration, one's commitment to physical fitness may hold significance; however, unless actively engaged in fitness-oriented endeavors, no progress is being made towards the realization of this objective. Consider any alternative pursuit that might be occupying the time that could otherwise be expended for maintaining optimal physical well-being, and substitute it accordingly.

Likewise, should you find yourself attending the cinema every Friday solely due to your friends' influence, yet recognize that your time could be better utilized elsewhere, it is advisable to gradually diminish your frequency of movie visits. Continuously minimize your engagement in futile endeavors in order to create space for pursuits that bring enrichment to your existence.

How to Teach Your Children That Less Is More

Have you ever found yourself strolling through a retail establishment, only to encounter a youngster persistently demanding various items? Is this an individual who feels compelled to handle every item on the shelves and incessantly expresses desire for each one? Alternatively, you may have encountered situations where you have been exposed to a disruptive child accompanied by a stressed parent who makes earnest attempts to pacify their child using various incentives, ranging from toys to confectionery items.

Perhaps, you were the parent who was overwhelmed and distressed. Perhaps you found yourself experiencing embarrassment and a sense of bewilderment regarding the appropriate course of action. Minimalism can help. It will not comprehensively address all of your parenting challenges. It cannot be definitively relied upon as a solution.

Nonetheless, it can provide you with valuable skills to effectively manage such incidents occurring within a retail environment. This could potentially prevent new parents from ever encountering such an experience.

For New Parents

As parents, our initial inclination, prior to even beholding the beauty of their gaze, is to provide our children with all the things they might require or desire. We desire to be fully equipped and ready for any potential eventualities that may arise. So we buy things. We engage in purchasing items of necessity, such as cribs and car seats, which we anticipate using.

We engage in the purchase of commodities that could potentially serve a purpose, as they possess an appealing aesthetic quality, such as toys and storage containers. As they age, we persist in exceeding reasonable limits.

We experience a sense of exhilaration upon witnessing their ability to assume an upright position, prompting us to provide them with chairs, bouncers, and walkers. Before long, your residence begins to resemble that of a household with numerous infants, despite the presence of just a single child.

This is the beginning. Before long, they amass such a multitude of toys that they no longer engage in play with them. They possess wardrobes comprising garments which are worn a single time before they become too small. We have already initiated them into a realm characterized by abundance.

As they transition into their toddler years, we misconstrue their signals. We acknowledge the need to undertake various tasks, and despite their fatigue, we persist in compelling them to do so. Subsequently, you find yourself positioned within the establishment, accompanied by a particularly restless young child, resorting to proffering various playthings, treats, or any other possible distractions in order to prolong the duration required for completing your essential errands. We have instilled in them the belief that the acquisition of goods directly corresponds to experiencing happiness.

Once they reach an age of understanding, they utilize this knowledge for their own benefit. The most straightforward approach to preventing this occurrence is by ensuring that it never initiates. Plan your days simply. They matter. Convey their significance by refraining from exerting pressure on them. It may entail occasional inconveniences, yet the ultimate outcome justifies them.

Four: The Factors Contributing to Disarray

I am confident that you have observed this occurrence within your own household, thus rendering a reminder unnecessary. However, should it have escaped your attention, clutter is indeed quite vexing. It accumulates within your residence, resulting in an untidy and cluttered appearance. On occasions, my residence appears as if I am an ardent collector of toys. It accumulates on your schedule, resulting in a rushed, overwhelmed, and fatigued state. And it accumulates within your interpersonal connections, encroaching upon your personal limits and compelling you to engage with individuals whom you should not be involved with.

The presence of clutter can be quite vexing, as it accumulates and depletes one's time, energy, and financial resources. Rather than having the freedom to allocate your resources towards the things that hold significant value to you, you are compelled to expend them on various insignificant expenditures that accumulate over time.

The complexities of clutter lie in the tendency for individuals to acclimate to its presence, thus rendering them oblivious to its existence. It accumulates discreetly until a certain moment when one finds oneself surveying their dwelling, contemplating the origins of all the possessions surrounding them. Subsequently, we indeed become motivated to declutter, a phenomenon that may temporarily mitigate the presence of clutter. Primarily, the act of collecting clutter is ingrained within us and occurs nearly automatically.

When contemplating the concept of clutter, our thoughts typically gravitate towards physical clutter - the small miscellaneous items that accumulate within the confines of our homes. Nonetheless, excess accumulation may also occur in various aspects of your life.

Calendar overcrowding

In addition to tangible disarray, one of the more exasperating forms of clutter pertains to the accumulation of excessive obligations on one's schedule. You have taken on a workload that exceeds your capacity in your professional role. It appears that you have meetings scheduled for the next two decades. Your daughter is actively involved in both the drama and choir programs, both of which are scheduled to hold performances on the same weekend. Your son is also a member of the choir, however, he will be unable to attend the scheduled performance this weekend due to his participation with the baseball team's travel arrangements. Additionally, he is a member of the basketball team. And potentially even among the ensemble. You are constantly endeavoring to synchronize schedules with your partner due to the unconventional work hours demanded by their job. Moreover, there is an individual within your social circle who persistently expresses the desire to engage in extensive phone conversations lasting for durations of three to four hours.

It is incredibly effortless for your calendar to become filled with excessive clutter. As your children mature, you desire their active participation in various school-affiliated endeavors. It constitutes an integral aspect of the high-school journey, does it not? However, when you incorporate all of these commitments into your already busy schedule of professional duties, social engagements, and familial responsibilities, you will inevitably find yourself with very limited availability to dedicate to the things that hold true significance for you.

Mental disarray

One may not give it much consideration, but it is possible for the mind to accumulate clutter just as easily as one's physical living space. If you have experienced the sensation of one's cognitive abilities deteriorating, it is likely attributed to the mental fatigue resulting from an excessive accumulation of mental clutter. To a certain extent, we are unable to prevent this. Our intellect is ceaselessly engaged, directing our physical actions, cautioning against perilous activities, and otherwise executing vital tasks essential for our everyday existence.

That constitutes a considerable quantity of items, and it persists incessantly, even during periods of sleep. Furthermore, when we consider the additional information and stimuli that we continuously feed our minds, they can rapidly transform into a perpetual maelstrom of commotion. The presence of mental clutter serves as a source of distraction, impairing our ability to concentrate on matters of significance to us. Moreover, in instances where our ability to concentrate is compromised, we have a greater propensity for recklessness and impulsivity in our judgments, resulting in unfavourable decisions that have the potential to impact various aspects of our existence such as interpersonal connections, time management, professional trajectories, vitality, and other spheres.

Days Three and Four, TheDecluttering Protocol

Now you possess a comprehensive comprehension of the objective at hand. You have meticulously crafted and selected lists, thereby enabling yourself to effectively carry out your meticulously devised plans. The time for further procrastination has come to an end; it is now imperative to establish clear guidelines and take personal responsibility for one's actions. Will the aforementioned list of desired items eventually find a new place of residence?

Please hold on momentarily, as the passage of time alone will not significantly impact the course of your life. Do not be distressed, as this is not an abrupt solution for overcoming your phobia. You are afforded a grace period of two days to gradually adapt to your newly organized and clutter-free lifestyle. In order to provide guidance and assistance, it is recommended that you designate one room within your household as an area devoid of clutter.

It is incumbent upon you to determine what can rightfully be left in that room, as no item may remain there unless it is deemed appropriate.

After selecting the room, it is imperative to promptly enter and proceed with the task of emptying it. It is possible to thoroughly cleanse the area and eliminate all objects, retaining only minimal furniture, the rug, and the wall paint; however, this approach would be quite jolting. Please acquire several boxes and inspect the contents of the aforementioned room.

Position a box at the center of the room and proceed to systematically gather all the items that have not been inspected or utilized within the preceding week, by traversing the entire space. If one does not engage in introspection regarding the essence of existence whilst observing that diminutive owl sculpture, it is advisable to place it within the container.

Thoroughly assess all of the belongings, and any items that are not used or enjoyed on a regular basis should be placed in the designated box.

After the completion of your initial survey of the room, proceed to seal the box and set it aside. By the time you have completed the task, it is conceivable that you will acquire a multitude of boxes. Prior to inspection, securely seal the boxes and affix appropriate labels for their transportation. You may opt to bring them to any thrift store or charitable organization that accepts donated used items.

If you have an intention to conduct a garage sale, ensure that you have a designated location to relocate the unsold items. One may also opt to vend them online; however, it is important to establish a finite duration for the selling endeavor.

With the passage of time, you will gradually acclimate to the absence of clutter in that room. Now you have come to perceive the insignificance of those items.

Indeed, while you may have initially found satisfaction in acquiring and placing those possessions within your living space, it is quite feasible to go about your life without the burden of infrequently utilized items.

Social Media Platforms Exert Psychological Influence

Is it possible to lead a life that is sheltered from the influence and disruptions caused by others? To accomplish this, it is imperative to possess an understanding of one's individual work style. One must adhere to the ancient wisdom that encourages individuals to have a comprehensive understanding of one's own self. Frequently, we exhibit a lack of proficiency in this area.

On the contrary, there are individuals who possess an insightful comprehension of our true nature. They possess awareness of our preferences, our cognitive capabilities, and any other ascertainable information derived from our Facebook user engagement. The devices that utilize this data gleaned from our interactions possess a deeper understanding of our personality than even our closest family and friends. It is only a matter of time before this form of artificial intelligence gains extensive knowledge about our identities. Our predicament lies in determining the most suitable manner of existence in light of the extensive knowledge that others possess about us.

Do we truly possess freedom today? Numerous enterprises are committed to acquiring and subsequently commercializing our focus; the most enticing lure they employ is social media. The emergence of popular social media platforms such as Twitter, Instagram, and Facebook has facilitated greater connectivity among individuals. However, there is a significant price to pay in both political and personal spheres for these actions. Users must assess whether the advantages obtained from these applications and websites merit the associated costs.

You must exercise independent judgment in reaching this decision. Is it possible for individuals to experience freedom in the presence of addictive nature of social media platforms? This is another decision that should be made based on a well-informed understanding. Is it possible that we are completely unaware of the identity of the individual operating from behind the curtain?

The initial founder of Facebook, Sean Parker, discussed the methodology employed during the site's conceptualization. Parked elucidated, "The primary consideration is how can we maximize the utilization of your time and conscious attention?"

In order to achieve this objective, it is imperative that users experience intermittent surges of dopamine resulting from receiving feedback such as likes or comments on their photos or posts, as this will significantly enhance their engagement.

He subsequently added, 'This represents the precise type of innovation that someone with my expertise in hacking would conceive, as it leverages a weakness in human psychology... The individuals responsible for its conception, the original architects, are none other than myself, Mark, and all of us possessed a conscious awareness of this.' Nevertheless, we proceeded with our course of action.

Build a Healthy Habit

We are capable of swiftly acquiring information on our electronic devices compared to the cumbersome pace of accumulating physical clutter. For this very reason, mere disposal of unnecessary information is insufficient and cannot be considered a comprehensive approach. It is imperative that you establish a consistent routine. It is imperative that you exhibit persistence and allocate a minimum of several minutes each day to undertake the task of decluttering and organizing your technological belongings.

Numerous individuals tend to neglect the process of clearing redundant files from their computer, phone, or tablet due to the seemingly limitless storage capacity, coupled with the continuous accumulation of information. Certain individuals deem it unworthy of their time to diligently undertake the task of sorting, organizing, and eliminating files and folders on a daily basis due to its excessively monotonous nature. The accumulation of digital clutter can rapidly escalate and occasionally evoke a sense of being inundated. Nevertheless, you have the ability to regain authority over the situation regardless of your perception of its severity.

To establish a constructive practice of arranging your devices and categorizing all the files and programs you possess, it is imperative to acquire comprehensive knowledge concerning various categories of digital disarray. It is imperative to acquire the ability to identify such individuals and to acquaint oneself with appropriate methods of engaging with them. Presented herein are the prevailing selections that perchance necessitate your attention:

The phenomenon of clutter resulting from the mindset of potential future utility: It is likely that you have already encountered this issue during the process of organizing your household belongings, and arriving at an optimal decision was invariably challenging. The widespread issue of envisaging potential future use for such items is known to have comparable consequences on the state of digital clutter. Individuals retain possessions due to the plausible occurrence of circumstances that necessitate their utilization. There is an absence of necessity to retain possessions, including files and programs, that are not required. As time progresses, the accumulation of files will accelerate to the point where your computer's performance is impaired and locating essential items becomes problematic. If a file is stored for future utilization, there is a strong probability of eventual oversight. Kindly consider deleting any unnecessary data, both for the sake of your technological resources and personal convenience.

Transient disarray: Its transience is deceptive, particularly in relation to technological apparatus. You possess an extraordinary capacity to accumulate information, which at times presents challenges in keeping pace with its influx. You encounter a variety of images, files, and downloads whose purpose is unknown to you, thus opting to postpone addressing them for the time being. Refrain from doing so! It is crucial to ascertain at this moment whether you are considering a matter of significance or not.

"What if?" is a question that often finds its way into the minds of individuals on numerous occasions. In this particular instance, the accumulation of digital clutter occurs as individuals exercise caution regarding the retention of information on the premise that it may prove indispensable at a later point in time. This category bears resemblance to the initial one, albeit with certain distinctions. You have already assimilated and applied this information, yet you hesitate to remove it. Certain clutter may include outdated projects in which you were once involved, giving rise to a recurring concern of potential future use. However, this mental state of apprehension is unfounded and ultimately contributes to a greater accumulation of clutter beyond one's perception. The accumulation of all this information occupying your thoughts will undeniably result in prolonged periods of distress and anxiety, spanning from days to weeks, or potentially even years. Eliminate any items or materials that are no longer necessary. Please refrain from fabricating hypothetical scenarios that may or may not come to pass. Reside in the current moment and embrace the tranquility of a well-structured computer system.

Obsolete information: Certain individuals possess a propensity to neglect obsolete software and retain it within their computer or mobile device largely due to the ample storage capacity at their disposal. This issue arises when confronted with any type of digital disarray. You essentially have boundless capacity. There is no need for any concern regarding the arrangement of shelves and closets. Nevertheless, the constant inundation with irrelevant data on a daily basis precipitates feelings of stress and induces fatigue. Enable your stimuli to unwind and remove any outdated elements. It is highly probable that anything that is not being maintained to remain current is rendered obsolete and no longer of relevance.

Correspondence via electronic mail and newsletters: Kindly recall the website that requested your subscription to their newsletter or daily email communication, in return for a modest discount on their offerings. You probably don't. Nevertheless, you are currently in receipt of daily or weekly electronic correspondences from various websites that you have previously subscribed to. This could pose a significant hindrance, as it may foster a tendency to regularly monitor your email, resulting in frequent interruptions to your concentration. Promptly discontinue your subscription to newsletters and emails, thus allowing your email account to have respite. You will be presented with a significantly reduced amount of information to handle and notably fewer distractions.

An Ideal Moment For Reorganizing Your Life: Purge Your Thoughts And Invigorate Your Spirit

*Start Sorting Out

Have you been experiencing a significant level of constraint? Do you find yourself burdened with an extensive workload, despite your diligent efforts, as the day elapses seemingly insufficient? It appears that you have amassed a significant amount of both material and immaterial clutter. You must effectively streamline your life in order to eliminate all forms of clutter. Therefore, what strategies exist for reclaiming one's life by eliminating mental and spiritual clutter? First and foremost, adhere to a straightforward principle in life - Discern what truly matters to you and eliminate everything else. Let's get started.

*Set priorities

Create a prioritization schedule to establish clear preferences and discern your desired outcomes. The act of streamlining one's life is closely associated with the mastery of prioritization.

*Abide to commitments

Compiling a comprehensive list of your priorities will aid you in focusing your attention on all of your obligations. By achieving proficiency in fulfilling your obligations, you will experience minimal occurrences wherein you feel overwhelmed due to failure to meet expectations placed upon you.

*Respect your time

You should be aware of the significance of your time. Analyze the allocation and utilization of your daily hours. The aim is to completely revamp and reconfigure your daily schedule. The greater your concentration on being in the designated location and performing the assigned tasks, the diminished level of stress you shall experience.

Four: Sustaining the Principles of Minimalism

The availability of additional space does not imply the need to promptly occupy the newly liberated area. Furthermore, this does not imply that you are obliged to replace each and every item that you have gotten rid of. Naturally, it is essential to substitute items that genuinely necessitate replacement; however, this principle does not extend to every single object. For instance, should you possess a total of 18 pairs of shoes but only actively utilize eight, and subsequently opt to dispose of the remaining ten, that concludes the matter. There is no necessity to replenish the ten pairs that were discarded with an additional ten pairs that you perceive as truly essential. Once again, restrict yourself solely to what is genuinely necessary.

Initially, there may be a compelling inclination to populate all available empty areas with aesthetically pleasing and brand-new items. Renovating and enhancing the aesthetic appeal of your recently purged area is an inherent inclination, particularly subsequent to the considerable decluttering efforts you have undertaken. While this concept presents a compelling and thrilling proposition, it is imperative to exercise caution and avoid the possibility of excessive accumulation that may surpass or match the quantity of items that have been disposed of. Keep in mind that your objective should be to embrace a minimalist lifestyle.

There may also be some initial challenges or resistance when attempting to declutter for the first time. With the passage of time, there is a noticeable increase in the sentimental worth assigned to old belongings, or a growing inclination to retain objects for potential future use manifests itself as each item is handled. This phase will ensue organically, yet it is essential to reflect upon the guidelines you have acquired to determine what ought to be eliminated.

In due time, particularly as you perceive a sense of liberation concerning your belongings and surroundings, you will seamlessly transition into a minimalist lifestyle with minimal resistance. As the embrace of minimalism increasingly becomes an integral part of your lifestyle, you will discern additional advantages beyond the joys of decluttering expounded upon in the preceding :

The mindset can be influenced by an environment that is simplified or characterized by minimalism. Due to the absence of distractions and the presence of only essential elements, one operates in a similar manner. When confronted with a task, you promptly undertake the requisite actions. You display a commendable level of attentiveness, demonstrating a heightened ability to maintain focus on the immediate tasks at hand, without succumbing to distractions.

The cognitive processes of individuals are significantly influenced by their immediate environment. When one's surroundings are organized and free of excess, it enhances cognitive clarity, facilitating the process of making sound decisions with greater ease and efficiency.

Due to your adherence to the principle of retaining only essentials, you possess a discerning ability to determine what should be acquired or added to your belongings. Consequently, you are more inclined to exhibit self-generosity, as you possess the ability to effectively manage your belongings. Additionally, should you exhibit magnanimity towards yourself, there exists no peril of excessive indulgence, for your discernment of your genuine necessities remains astute. This signifies that even when indulging in luxuries, one can responsibly uphold the equilibrium demanded by a minimalist way of life.

You exhibit enhanced clarity and assuredness in terms of discerning your requirements and effectively overseeing your expenditures. Once more, it should be noted that minimalism does not involve leading a meager existence. It pertains primarily to being aware of the destinations of one's financial resources, ensuring that they are allocated to endeavors of substantial value. Therefore, although the initial cost may be higher, investing in high-quality exercise equipment is a wise choice due to the considerable time you will spend utilizing it daily, in contrast to purchasing a more affordable alternative that does not provide the same level of enjoyment.

As one acclimates to a minimalist lifestyle, there is a noticeable readiness of both the body and mind to readily adjust to it. Therefore, in the event that you happen to deviate from the process of decluttering and maintaining a simplified environment, your emotional well-being and physical state will serve as indicators. You may experience a decrease in energy, a decline in mood, or mild physical discomfort. In this particular situation, it is advisable to implement a decluttering process, or at the very least, organize and tidy up one of the areas in which you commonly reside. Evidently, it can be deduced that minimalism equally contributes to one's mental and emotional well-being in addition to their physical well-being. An illuminated and airy atmosphere contributes to fostering a serene and composed mental and physical state.

Adopt a more deliberate approach in order to achieve efficiency and effectiveness in a timely manner.

Occasionally, it is necessary to decelerate in order to accelerate efficiently.

JEFF OLSON

I

During one of his interviews, Tom Morello recounts a compelling anecdote from his formative years as a dedicated guitarist. He was endeavoring to master rapid guitar solos, and that was his means of impressing those who were attentive. He rendezvoused with one of his instructors, who happens to be renowned as one of the most accomplished guitarists on the global stage. Tom attempted to perform these rapid solos in order to make a favorable impression on him. The instructor attentively lent an ear to his words and advised him to moderate his pace. As per his analysis, the sole approach to executing rapid solos with precision entails starting with an impeccably played slow rendition, becoming proficient at that pace, and thereafter gradually augmenting the tempo to maintain the same unwavering level of accuracy.

Upon initially encountering this piece of guidance, I was taken aback due to its seemingly paradoxical nature. We regard swiftness as an indication of proficiency, and hereby present a suggestion that urges you to moderate your pace as a means to attain expertise.

This principle is applicable in all domains. The majority of errors occurring in computer programs stem from individuals attempting to utilize exceedingly complex constructs without possessing a genuine comprehension of them. Hence, it is recommended to initiate the utilization of more straightforward elements, deliberately experimenting with them before incorporating them into a more intricate framework. It is advisable for founders within startup ventures to personally manage essential tasks, acquire a comprehensive understanding of each aspect, and subsequently delegate them to others to accelerate progress. It appears that the most opportune moment to minimize errors lies in the early stages of the process, during a period of low intensity. When the initial steps are relatively free of errors, it is probable that the subsequent stages will also exhibit a reduced likelihood of errors.

In our pursuit of financial independence, this principle advises us to commence our journey on the investment pathway with caution and moderation. There exist several fundamental principles and behaviors in accordance with this.

MINIMALIST HOME DECLUTTERING HABITS

Now that you have acquired comprehension of the concept of minimalism, comprehended its benefits for you, and identified potential applications in your life, you are now poised to embark upon your journey towards minimalist living. Commence the process by embracing these minimalist practices:

MINIMALIST HOME DECLUTTERING HABITS

Disarray pervades every corner, and this perpetual accumulation of disarray can be regarded as the fundamental composition of most households. However, this need not be the scenario within the confines of your personal dwelling, particularly when armed with these efficacious strategies to tackle clutter. In the near future, you will find yourself immersed in the tranquil elegance of your well-organized abode.

Ready…

1. Set forth your objectives for organizing your living space.

It is imperative to establish a comprehensive plan before commencing the decluttering process for your home.

A crucial initial step in developing this plan involves clearly articulating your goals. To initiate your progress, it is beneficial to keep the following points in consideration:

• Compile a comprehensive inventory or construct a diagram encompassing all chambers and gathering spots of disarray within your domicile.

• Allocate a suitable duration to each area within your residence by assigning a rating based on the extent of disarray.

• Elect to address one area or chamber in a sequential manner.

• Determine achievable deadlines for the completion of each phase of your decluttering objectives. Please ensure that the selected dates are feasible; incorporating a certain level of challenge may potentially contribute to enhancing the experience of decluttering, making it more enjoyable rather than burdensome.

Five: Success Story

As a mother who is employed and resides in New York City, the condition of my household can easily be envisioned. While I wouldn't label myself as pretentious, who wouldn't appreciate the pleasure of wearing impeccably washed and coordinated socks on a daily basis? The yearning to don pristine, coordinated socks propelled me to seek out literature and scholarly publications that would aid me in maintaining pristine order in both my abode and existence. Serendipitously, I stumbled upon Marie Kondo's book and it undeniably transformed my life. Upon reading her book on two separate occasions within a short span of time, I came to the realization that her methodology possessed the potential to aid me in my pursuit of leading an orderly existence, thus commencing my expedition towards a life of organization.

I will be engaging in falsehood if I were to express that I did not feel apprehensive about the idea of organizing by categories. The undertaking itself is colossal, yet it proved particularly arduous for me due to the added responsibility of monitoring my three young children concurrently. By some means I succeeded, however, the most challenging aspect still lay ahead. I do not engage in hoarding behavior; rather, I prefer to diligently preserve items for future purposes.

Kondo's disapproval of hoarding contradicts my beliefs, yet I had already resolved to adhere to her methodology, and thus I persevered. After several attempts, I achieved success, and it dawned on me that the approach was indeed effective. Consequently, both my wardrobe and life became thoroughly decluttered and significantly more organized. I highly endorse this approach for individuals seeking to experience a simplified and serene lifestyle.

3: Aspects to Take into Account

It is relatively straightforward (and can even be enjoyable, once you find your rhythm) to engage in the process of physically decluttering your residence. The challenge lies in maintaining an organized state after eliminating the clutter and resuming regular activities. Academic assignments begin accumulating within folders designated for future reference, toys are retrieved by well-intentioned grandparents, and miscellaneous items have a tendency to inadvertently make their way into your residence. In a shopping bag.That you are in possession of (although it was required).

Developing guidelines for your family may be perceived as a tedious aspect of this entire process, nevertheless, it is undeniably one of the most crucial measures you can take to ensure the sustained elimination of clutter. An initial and paramount principle that can be established for your family is that which pertains to expressing gratitude.

Express gratitude for the things you possess.

It is highly recommended that you opt for prominently displaying a set of guidelines for your entire family to observe on a daily basis (which is strongly advised). Among these guidelines, prioritizing this particular one should be paramount. I am uncertain about your situation, but in my case, I am experiencing a phase with my preschooler where he tends to exhibit ingratitude towards his possessions. On a certain day, my parents made a purchase of a toy for him. Yet, on the following day, he expresses to me that the aforementioned toy has become outdated and he is in need of a replacement. Although the childish tone of his three-year-old voice may elicit some endearing feelings, it also proves exasperating. This holds true for many aspects involving a resolute three-year-old, as I am discovering - they possess an endearing yet vexing quality.

In that particular instance, his adeptness at expressing gratitude may have been inconspicuous, yet he possesses commendable proficiency in conveying appreciation when others perform actions on his behalf. But that's another story.

The essence of my argument is this: under no circumstances would I have ever deliberately imparted such behavior to my child. Although I may have engaged in such behavior on occasion, I believe it to be a common human predisposition as well. We aspire to improve ourselves, acquire greater resources, and engage in more impressive endeavors, and this determination is not necessarily detrimental. Additionally, it plays a crucial role in our personal development and enables us to make positive contributions to society.

If left unaddressed, however, it may also result in a sense of entitlement, dissatisfaction, and disorder.

It is crucial to instruct our children in cultivating a sense of gratitude for their possessions, as this will minimize their inclination to incessantly pursue materialistic acquisitions. A method to initiate the process of instilling gratitude in your children is to regularly engage in the act of expressing gratitude to one another on a daily basis. Irrespective of the time of day, such as during breakfast, dinner, or prior to sleep, kindly gather your family members and request each person to express their gratitude by sharing one or two aspects they are thankful for. The key lies in avoiding anything of a general nature, such as one's family, residence, belongings, and so forth. It is imperative that the declaration of gratitude provided is both precise in nature and accompanied by a comprehensive explanation of the underlying reason. In addition, it is worth noting that this applies not only to your children. You and your partner are encouraged to partake in the activity as well! It is important for us, as adults, to acknowledge that we can sometimes fall prey to ingratitude and dissatisfaction, much like our children. Therefore, it becomes imperative that we cultivate the ability to shift our attention towards appreciating what we already possess.

An alternative approach is to alter your expressions from "I want..." to "I have...". When you or your partner or your children express a desire by stating "I want," it is advisable to interrupt and request them to rephrase it using the phrase "I have." In the event that your child expresses a desire for a new toy, encourage them to articulate appreciation for something they already possess. Alternatively, in a formal tone: "In the event that you find yourself uttering, 'I desire this exquisite new coat,' pause and recollect the coat that you presently possess." It is likely that it performs equally effectively as it did in the previous year, when your level of excitement matched that which you currently have for this new coat.

The Many Benefits Of Practising Less

Naturally, it is impossible to precisely ascertain the beneficial outcomes that may arise from adopting a minimalist lifestyle. Nevertheless, it is a verifiable reality that it can yield numerous benefits. I will provide a more comprehensive elucidation of these benefits in the subsequent .

More money

Naturally, it is contingent upon the lifestyle and life path one selects. Upon embracing a particular lifestyle, a discernible advantage in terms of financial well-being can be observed.

While finances do not hold considerable significance within minimalist lifestyles, it would be beneficial to accumulate savings. For instance, one allocates financial resources towards significant aspects of life while refraining from excessive indebtedness, and potentially eschews the acquisition of lavish automobiles or residences. This leads to an automatic reduction in costs and eliminates a portion of the expenses. In the absence of an automobile, the motor vehicle insurance policy would be terminated and there would be no need to incur expenses associated with fuel consumption. The expenses related to workshop services for car repairs are also excluded, resulting in significant cost savings. I firmly believe that adopting a minimalist lifestyle would undoubtedly yield financial benefits. What factors could exacerbate the current situation?

Happy

Fortune undoubtedly plays a significant role in one's disposition. Additionally, there exist various variables that are incalculable. By embracing a minimalist lifestyle, you are enhancing the likelihood of experiencing increased happiness in your life. There exists a straightforward explanation for that. Through the adoption of a minimalist lifestyle, one's life is emancipated. You are relieved of various superfluous elements and primarily unburdened by any extraneous weight. There is a higher likelihood of you regaining a comprehensive understanding of the situation. Possessions entail a significant amount of responsibility, and the greater one's ownership, the greater the corresponding responsibility becomes.

Furthermore, the greater the extent of one's possessions, the higher the magnitude of potential loss. As the potential losses increase, so too does the corresponding escalation of the fear of loss. However, once you have rid yourself of superfluous possessions, it becomes apparent that you require minimal resources to experience contentment and joy. Due to the reduction in the number of elements under consideration, there arises a heightened focus on matters of significant import. As one matures, reminiscences and life encounters gain significance, with an increased focus on personal liberty and cherished relationships, while concurrently diminishing the prominence of stress and responsibilities.

Grateful

You will possess a decreased quantity of belongings, yet your level of gratitude will amplify. By focusing solely on the fundamental aspects of existence, one becomes cognizant that their life is no longer governed by countless routines and behaviors. You maintain a comprehensive perspective on your life, enabling heightened awareness and the deliberate appreciation of moments. You will have the opportunity to express greater gratitude. Appreciative of all your possessions and equally appreciative of the things you lack. Expressing deep appreciation for the individuals who hold immense significance in one's life. I am deeply appreciative for the blessings of joy, good health, and the cherished moments that life bestows upon me. Grateful for life.

ease

You will also derive advantages from adopting a minimalist lifestyle when you relocate or engage in travel. It will become evident to you that you lack a precise understanding of what items to bring, and upon relinquishing control, you will experience an unsettling sensation of having overlooked something. The process of making these choices becomes significantly simplified with the adoption of a minimalist lifestyle. Due to the presence of a smaller quantity of items, you are also capable of providing responses to the inquiries with greater ease.

What items are necessary for me to bring along?

What is the appropriate method for storing it?

What is the required number of suitcases?

One becomes aware that minimalism entails reducing possessions, resulting in decreased stress.

What is the extent of time and energy allocated to engaging with social media attractions?

The significant investment of time and effort made towards ephemeral interests within the realm of social media concisely illustrates its considerable influence over us. This grip is magnified when individuals grapple with or encounter challenges in disengaging from the displays of their mobile phones, personal computers, or any other technological apparatus. Our freedom becomes compromised when we are susceptible to the influence of these digital devices. It is rather ironic that the subject or entity intended to bestow us with a certain degree of liberty ultimately results in the forfeiture of our autonomy. Social media serves as a pervasive means for asserting our human rights whenever they are infringed upon by individuals or governing entities. Nonetheless, it has also assumed an unprecedented level of influence and influence in virtually every facet of our existence, giving rise to a novel form of dependence.

Individuals who are held captive by this emerging compulsion relinquish their autonomy while falsely perceiving themselves to be in command. They consistently rely excessively on the internet as a source of ideas and opinions, beyond a level that can be considered conducive to a healthy approach. This contemporary phenomenon of addiction encompasses individuals from diverse racial backgrounds and across all age groups, provided that they possess the ability to read and write. The perceived utility of social media is excessively magnified and unduly relied upon, with a discernible instinct within us alerting us to the emergence of addictive patterns. However, this perception is frequently disregarded or considered an inevitable consequence.

The undeniable fact is that we are aware when we excessively engage in a specific task, yet instead of making adaptations, we mistakenly associate this "excessive focus" with utility.

Gaining comprehension of the factors that contribute to a recreational pursuit is an exceptionally crucial and subjectively influenced perspective. The concept of social media may be categorized by certain groups of individuals as a recreational pursuit, while other individuals or groups may hold contrasting views on this matter. Engagement in social media has been established as a recognized source of income, however, exceeding certain limits can necessitate an intervention. Therefore, when regarding digital engagement as a form of recreation, it is essential to acknowledge the need for organization and to acknowledge the existence of alternative pastimes and hobbies for amusement. By adopting this approach, no recreational activity is exerting complete control over an individual's focus, thereby creating opportunities for progress and advancement in different domains.

Assessing the duration of our captivation with social media allurements entails appraising the extent of time expended or utilized in engaging with the phone, laptop, or any electronic apparatus through swiping and scrolling. Engaging in a health-oriented digital minimalist lifestyle necessitates a careful evaluation of the trade-offs between time expenditure and anticipated advantages. It concerns the identification of responses to inquiries such as- Within this limited timeframe, what achievements did I accomplish? Throughout this considerable duration, my attention has been captivated by various forms of media entertainment. Consequently, one cannot help but inquire about the accomplishments that I have attained during this period.

Understanding the opportunity cost of digital influence is equivalent to recognizing the expenditure of personal energy, interests, and time it entails. One could equally devote their time to a more significant pursuit, merely requiring the discernment to identify which undertaking holds greater importance, namely, which endeavor is deserving of one's time, exertion, and remains unaffected by external factors such as social influence.

Behaviors driven by a compulsion, such as mindlessly engaging in social media platforms like Instagram or TikTokwhile simultaneously watching a film, demonstrate a significant association with challenges related to memory recall and diminished ability to sustain focus. According to research conducted at Stanford University in California, these patterns of behavior appear to have an impact on a cognitive function called "episodic memory."

The mean duration and effort dedicated to social media among distinct generations have undergone a disconcerting transformation. A significant factor contributing to this issue is the deliberate design of the social media user experience, which fosters increased and compulsive usage. A conventional demonstration of this assertion can be observed in the examination of Instagram, a widely recognized international community. In the past, the utilization of Instagram presented an experience that greatly diverges from the current state; subsequent to the introduction of additional features, newer and improved iterations of the Instagram application have emerged. Nowadays, there are additional gratifying elements such as social media engagements like likes, hashtags, and comments, which foster a heightened level of participation. These numerous diversions consistently disrupt an individual's tranquility throughout the day, thus intensifying the compulsion to incessantly monitor each undertaking.

Andrew Sullivan authored a lengthy seven-thousand-word essay for New York magazine entitled "I Used to Be a Human Being." The accompanying subtitle of the piece resonated deeply, conveying the profound impact of our incessant exposure to news, gossip, and imagery, rendering us trapped in a ceaseless cycle of information consumption as compulsive addicts. It broke me. "It has the potential to also cause you harm." He is a prominent and highly influential online content creator. The in-depth examination of the sentiment and power expressed in this piece of literature will be addressed in detail in the following subsection.

Social Advantages

Despite being primarily an individual lifestyle choice, the minimalist lifestyle brings forth numerous societal benefits. As an advocate of minimalism, you have the capacity to provide assistance to others in various areas. In the first place, residing in a meticulously organized residence imparts a favorable initial perception to visiting acquaintances, portraying you as an individual with a keen penchant for orderliness and cleanliness. Such an impression is likely to ignite an innate inspiration within them, prompting a desire to emulate your esteemed way of life. Who among us does not appreciate the act of inspiring others? The serenity and tranquility emanated by your minimalist way of life will inevitably arouse curiosity, leading others to inquire about the methods you employed to achieve such a state. In truth, every individual on this planet aspires to live a more affluent, harmonious, and dynamic existence. And you simply exhibit them a glimpse of that. That\\\'s quite inspirational.

In addition, should you have a family and children, you become a lifelong source of educational wisdom for them. By adopting this approach, you have the ability to influence the trajectory of your children's futures and assist them in acquiring the skills necessary to make judicious choices expeditiously. Furthermore, they will be raised in an environment that prioritizes the significance of human beings and their encounters over material possessions. By raising children in this manner, you are making a commendable contribution to society.

You may also make a valuable contribution to the elimination of poverty in our society through the donation of any surplus items you possess. While it might represent an excess or surplus to your circumstances, it could potentially hold immense significance, potentially even determining life or death, for another individual. Upon embarking on the decluttering process, you will undoubtedly be astounded by the realization that numerous items have been needlessly squandered. Therefore, bestowing your possessions upon individuals who are in need will represent your equitable contribution to the enhancement of society and the promotion of egalitarianism among individuals. This exemplifies the immense potential that minimalism holds. Moreover, your noble act will initiate a domino effect of benevolent actions, thereby reinstating people's faith in the inherent goodness of humanity. Our society is currently facing a pressing necessity for precisely that.

A compelling advantage of embracing minimalism is the renewed emphasis it places on cherished relationships. You shall not accord greater importance to anything above your family and friends. This will engender a highly favorable transformation in your existence, as well as in the lives of your cherished acquaintances. Consequently, society will benefit from the favorable impact generated by you and your family. The available time and energy that will be at your disposal will prove highly advantageous for your loved ones. In the unfortunate event of your demise, your children shall be spared the arduous task of meticulously organizing an extensive inventory of belongings. This implies that even after your demise, you will continue to benefit them positively. It evokes a sense of unease, yet remains fundamentally optimistic. Your fervor and enthusiasm will imbue your loved ones and acquaintances alike.

According to popular belief, individuals of virtuous character tend to gravitate towards others who possess similar positive traits. When you emanate positive energy towards society, society reciprocates with amplified benevolence. The positive contributions you make to society are reciprocated in numerous manners. It entails reciprocity, but the onus is on you to take the lead. Your inclination towards leading a minimalist personal life has the potential to contribute significantly to the establishment of a minimalist society, a pursuit that embodies the ultimate aspiration of any given society. Once the broader society embraces minimalism, the issues inherent in our cultures will naturally dissipate, and the interplay between societies will facilitate the adoption of a minimalist way of life by other societies and cultures. Fundamentally, you initiate a cascading process by engaging in a self-serving act.

Recommendation #15: Limit the Use of Electronic Devices

In contemporary society, a substantial number of individuals possess multiple electronic devices. Various electronic devices such as cell phones, music devices, computers, television sets, cable boxes, video game devices, and others are acquired and subsequently placed in different locations within the residence. Kitchen appliances such as blenders, slow cookers, microwave ovens, toaster ovens, and other compact devices are also accumulated. These items have a tendency to occupy significant amounts of space and incur substantial expenses. In numerous instances, objects such as cell phones, televisions, video game systems, and computers are consuming financial resources even when not in active utilization. We have equipped them with monthly subscription services that grant us extensive data, as well as the ability to procure games, television programs, music, and other related content. Upon honest examination of our electronic devices, it is highly probable that we possess only a select few that we hold in higher regard while the remaining devices remain idle, accumulating dust and squandering financial resources.

To optimize the utilization of your financial resources, time, and physical space, it is advisable to minimize the presence of electronic devices. Retain possessions with versatile functionality, and discard those lacking such capabilities. It is unnecessary to possess a tablet, computer, music device, and cell phone. Instead, retain possession of your cellular device and personal computer while relinquishing ownership of the remaining items. In the majority of instances, we possess an excessive number of electronic devices primarily due to their aesthetic appeal and the perceived value of a few additional functions they offer. In actuality, their presence is nonessential and they merely occupy physical space and entail financial expenditure.

Recommendation #16: Universally Applicable

Consolidating items into universally applicable or versatile items is a highly advantageous strategy to diminish the quantity of possessions while retaining their inherent value. Take into account an example such as a versatile hammer that also functions as multiple tools. At numerous hardware retail establishments, one can procure a versatile tool that serves the dual purpose of a hammer and a screwdriver, and possibly even includes pliers. Consequently, you have the ability to reduce the number of tools and tool bits in your possession and instead retain a singular item. With the possession of that item, you can achieve any objective of your desire, and its storage poses utmost convenience. There is no necessity for possessing an extensive assortment of tools, as a solitary tool would suffice.

Your household possesses numerous objects that can be consolidated in order to fulfill a singular function. One can discover a range of kitchen utensils, bathroom accessories, storage units, and miscellaneous appliances that possess a multifunctional nature, thereby enabling the consolidation of multiple individual items into a single entity. This particular item is akin to a utopian vision for individuals who embrace a minimalist lifestyle.

Examination Of Minimalism In Comparison To Consumerism

In recent decades, the ideology of minimalism has progressively garnered momentum, emerging as a prominent term in both digital and physical spaces. What exactly is minimalism? What factors contribute to its growing popularity and significance? What benefits can be derived from embracing a minimalist lifestyle?

Minimalism creates an environment that fosters the presence of only the essentials.

Certain individuals may hold preexisting beliefs concerning the concept of minimalism. They hold the belief that it signifies relinquishment and hardship. When considering minimalism, individuals may associate it with ideals of austerity, Zen philosophy, or various religious and spiritual practices. Alternatively, they may consider minimalist art, architecture, and fashion. Certain individuals may perceive minimalism as monotonous and lackluster, prompting them to adopt maximalism as a countermeasure. In the meantime, there exists a faction that criticizes minimalism as excessively austere, asserting that individuals ought to pursue a lifestyle characterized by moderation and a penchant for simplicity.

All of these perspectives on minimalism are characterized by their extremity. While their arguments are not entirely without merit, it is important to note that they offer a somewhat limited perspective on the true nature of minimalism.

Fundamentally, minimalism entails a cognitive and behavioral approach that encourages individuals to introspect their lives and way of living, discerning what is truly necessary, and relinquishing anything superfluous in order to create room for genuine heartfelt aspirations. Minimalism embodies the principles of temperance and uncomplicated existence. The pursuit involves achieving equilibrium, with the heart serving as the pivotal point.

Let us employ analogical reasoning to enhance our understanding of this concept. When contrasting minimalism with health, it is evident that minimalism does not entail indulgence or sporadic dieting, but rather reflects the adoption of a wholesome and well-balanced way of life. When employing the analogy of finance, minimalism can be described as a practice of prudent financial allocation rather than wastefulness or miserliness. Finally, when considering childrearing, it does not entail either condescension or abandonment towards one's children, but rather involves granting them autonomy to develop and prosper within society.

As evidenced by these illustrations, minimalism necessitates a delicate equilibrium. It places emphasis on gain rather than loss, on the constructive rather than the adverse. It represents not a limitation, but rather an embodiment of liberty. Liberation from the perpetual cycle of consumerism, excess possessions, financial liabilities, diversions, commotion, and shallow associations.The liberty to prioritize interpersonal connections, well-being, contentment, prosperity, and the pursuit of one's personal calling and purpose in life.

The utilization of metaphors further exemplifies how minimalism extends across various dimensions of existence. An individual could embark on adopting a minimalist lifestyle initially focused on the decluttering of physical surroundings, but may experience the minimalist philosophy permeating various aspects of their existence, encompassing matters of personal well-being, finances, and familial relationships.

It appears that when one embraces the concept of minimalism wholeheartedly, it becomes evident in various aspects of their life. It inherently causes a transformation within oneself, leading to the incorporation of its principles into one's everyday existence.

In summary, the initial definition of minimalism entails transcending any misconceptions surrounding this concept, as it involves returning to the fundamental nature of objects and directing attention towards the core necessities. It is not merely a matter of creating vacant space for the sake of it. It is creating room for the necessary items. Upon embarking on this endeavor, one may discover that it is not a singular, momentous occurrence; rather, minimalism unfolds as an ongoing process, not merely an endpoint, but a means to accomplish personal ambitions. And you may discover that its positive impacts resonate across every facet of your existence.

However, the adoption of minimalism is not a passive occurrence. It is imperative that you ensure its realization. You must wholeheartedly devote yourself to it. It is imperative that you select minimalism. This leads us to the second interpretation of minimalism as a mentality and preference in one's way of life.

Minimalism for Your Family

If one is not single and residing alone, adopting minimalism as a lifestyle may pose considerable challenges. Initially, it is imperative to persuade your family members regarding the matter at hand. That will indisputably necessitate numerous significant deliberations, instances of conflict, and even emotional distress involving your children (or parents...or sister...or yourself). The initial phase entails the removal of all nonessential belongings from your residence. There may be disagreements regarding certain points, but ultimately, you should make decisions based on your own judgment. By doing so, you and your family as a whole will discover fresh avenues to allocate your time, resources, and financial means towards endeavors that hold paramount significance to each of you, both individually and collectively.

Not only that, however. You will develop a heightened sense of awareness regarding the manner in which our possessions encroach upon your cherished liberties and disrupt the strong familial connection. The most challenging aspect will arise when various things, regardless of their nature or form, begin to enter your households. It could initiate with the acquisition of collectible items and culminate in the complete occupation of a child's room. You must exert considerable effort to promptly address and prevent any relapses, and endeavor to restore a state of simplicity.

Therefore, it will be necessary for you to diligently exert effort in eliminating any excess objects or disarray that may accumulate in and around your residence, automobile, and thought processes.

Presented below are a handful of locations to initiate your cleaning and minimalist decluttering endeavors. This location serves as an excellent point of initiation!

Junk Mail

In the majority of households, approximately half of the correspondence received is comprised of unsolicited materials and advertisements that hold no significance or relevance to one's requirements. It typically remains in a stagnant state until, several months later, you either sift through it or dispose of it all at once. Promptly dispose of unsolicited mail in a designated recycling container and explore the possibility of discontinuing further receipt of such correspondence. Please pay attention to the organic influx of mail to your residence. Are you observing a significant number of credit card applications addressed to a particular individual? Should applications be received on a regular basis, please contact the aforementioned company for further assistance. You will be actively benefiting yourself while also contributing to environmental conservation by conveniently positioning a recycling receptacle in your kitchen or entryway. This strategic placement will effectively intercept a substantial portion of unsolicited mail, preventing it from cluttering your surfaces such as counters, tables, or desks. In addition, you will also observe a reduction in the amount of time spent sifting through it. Consequently, you will cease the wastage of your valuable time.

Check counter space

Ensure that kitchen appliances are stored discreetly. The sole deviation from this rule perhaps could pertain to your coffee apparatus. However, it is unnecessary to have toasters, blenders, food processors, and mixers occupying space on your kitchen countertops. Firstly, it is unhygienic, thus significantly complicating the process of cleaning. If the locations for your appliances remain unchanged for an extended period, it may be prudent to consider disposing of them. Additionally, it is worth considering the acquisition of multifunctional appliances that possess the capability to perform two or three distinct tasks. It is redundant to possess both a toaster oven and a toaster, as their functionalities largely overlap and render one another nearly obsolete.

Get to those closets

Please remove a total of 10 garments from your wardrobe today. It is highly probable that you can engage in a process of mentally organizing your belongings within your closet, all while remaining in your current location. Your prom dress is no longer necessary/appropriate or suitable for your current circumstances. Your previous workout attire ceased to accommodate your body when you discontinued your excrcise routine. Assuming you possess average attributes, it is expected that you can allocate approximately 5 minutes of your time to gather 10 articles of attire that are no longer utilized and subsequently place them within a container. Please ensure that this task is performed for each member residing in your household. Children's clothing will be the most effortless to gather, as it is the category with the highest accumulation. Your remaining garments will be more appropriately stored within your wardrobe. Your wardrobe storage will regain proper ventilation, enabling you to efficiently select your attire. Additionally, by labeling the container with "Goodwill" upon completion, you will experience a sense of personal satisfaction as soon as you deliver it. It is highly probable that you will experience a sense of inspiration that will prompt you to repeat the action.

A fulfilling occupation" or "A job that brings profound satisfaction

Resigning from employment is always a complex process.

I had been there. I resigned from my position at the multinational corporation several years ago in order to establish a tranquil life in my hometown.

No, it was not imposed by external coercion. It was solely intended for my own self and not for any other individuals. It discerned that it did not align well with my circumstances. I sought tranquility, I yearned for steadfastness, and above all, I longed to be reunited with my Family. The priorities I held upon my initial enrollment differed from my present perspectives. I had no desire to persist merely as a participant in the relentless pursuit of success.

Should you have formed preconceptions about me, perceiving me as feeble or lacking ambition concerning my professional pursuits, I feel compelled to inform you that I embarked upon a journey away from my place of origin immediately upon commencing my collegiate studies, spanning a duration of seven years and encompassing five distinct municipalities.

Arriving at this decision was not straightforward, given that I had previously held the belief that leaving my job would render my educational investment futile. I harbored anxiety regarding the potential emotional impact on my parents, who have made significant sacrifices for the advancement of my career. However, there was a single juncture where all progress came to a halt - the question of my own happiness.

Surprisingly, I have successfully secured an employment opportunity within the span of a month, which conveniently happens to be located in my hometown. As anticipated, the position entailed a different scope of responsibilities, the benefits package was diminished, and the prestigious multinational corporation association was no longer attached. Nonetheless, I willingly embraced the job opportunity, and now, four years later, I find myself content and thriving.

I am not suggesting that individuals should universally abandon their employment in pursuit of happiness.

However, my central argument is this: one should not allow their occupation to deprive them of contentment. It pertains to the act of decision-making. What holds greater significance in your view? What is your order of precedence in your personal life? What do you anticipate or aspire to achieve in your life?

Work for fixed hours

or Work flexibly

More Money

or More leisure time

Owning a big House

or renting a space

and most importantly,

Engage in employment to sustain your affluent way of life

Or Work for freedom

I am currently employed, however, the nature of my occupation does not sufficiently deplete my energy, thereby preventing me from feeling exhausted at the conclusion of each day. The purpose of Minimalism in our professional lives is to prompt us to reflect on our overall satisfaction with the majority of our workday, and the trade-off we make by sacrificing time that could be better spent with our family or pursuing our personal passions.

Does your occupation result in a sense of contentment or fatigue by the conclusion of each week? Do you happen to be employed in a particularly monotonous and demoralizing office occupation?

I desire for my life to encompass more than simply acquiring funds for consumption, but rather to acquire funds in order to dedicate substantial time to my other endeavors.

6: LESS DEBT

Numerous individuals engage in financial practices where they expend funds that have not been legitimately accrued, for acquiring items of negligible value, solely to make an impression on individuals with whom they hold no genuine affinity.

- Will Rogers

Debt pertains to the monetary obligations incurred by an individual to external parties or financial institutions.

This indicates that although you have immediate possession of the funds, they ultimately do not belong to you and must be returned to their rightful owner or the financial institution.

When considering the concept of debt, it can be classified into two distinct categories: beneficial debt and detrimental debt. Our primary objective is to address the issue of bad debt associated with this book, as it is our intention to diminish its prevalence. For those seeking further insights into the concept of beneficial debt, we kindly advise to anticipate forthcoming publications wherein this subject matter will be presented.

A thought-provoking concept, often misconstrued, pertains to the notion that the ownership of an item acquired through financial borrowing, be it a real estate property, an automobile, or even a technological device such as a phone or computer, is not realized until the associated debt is fully discharged. Have you devoted a sufficient amount of time to peruse the detailed terms and conditions? The object in question serves as the guarantee for your financial obligation. Thus, in the event of mortgage non-payment, the bank reserves the right to seize your property and subsequently sell it. It had not yet become your possession. Upon completion of the final payment, it shall be deemed rightfully yours.

A few days ago, I engaged in a conversation with a legal professional regarding this matter. According to the lawyer, even upon receiving a contract from a telecommunications company for a phone, such as an iPhone, the legal ownership of the device remains with the company until the completion of payment. Discuss the intricate details!

That is the reason why, in the case of a 24-month cell phone contract, a penalty must be paid if one chooses to terminate it prior to the designated duration. They are not requesting payment for the cancellation of the service per se, but rather for the remaining balance on the phone.

The allure of debt fades when the time for repayment arrives, which is why many individuals acquire credit cards and indulge in spending until they exhaust the card's limit. The most advisable course of action, provided one is devoid of debt and not compelled to acquire it for a substantial and pressing purpose, is to refrain from engaging in it. If you are contemplating obtaining a credit card, it is advisable to do so only if you are absolutely certain that you will be able to settle the outstanding balance in its entirety by the conclusion of each billing cycle. Ensure that the interest rate is also feasible, as certain credit card providers impose interest rates as high as 30%.

If one is free from debt, it is advisable to strive towards establishing a contingency fund. Based on the findings by Bankrate, a staggering 61% of the American population does not possess the financial means to cover an unexpected expense amounting to $1,000. It is recommended that your contingency reserve should encompass a minimum of $1,000. After attaining an adequate amount in your emergency fund, commence efforts towards accumulating savings that equate to six months' worth of expenses. In the event of any unforeseen circumstances leading to the loss of your primary source of income, you will be provided with financial assistance for a limited duration to sustain yourself until you devise a suitable course of action, such as securing new employment or establishing an alternative means of generating income. There is no greater distress than experiencing a severe financial need and lacking the means to obtain it. Individuals experience increasing desperation and consequently engage in irrational behavior as a means to obtain the necessary funds to sustain themselves throughout the month. These behaviors may potentially culminate in unlawful actions, namely, theft or the distribution of illicit substances.

It is comprehensible that there are occasions when we must opt for indebtedness, particularly in the event of unforeseen circumstances. This occurs when we fail to adequately plan for such expenses, leading to potential long-term financial ramifications. By establishing a savings buffer of at least $1,000 to handle unexpected emergencies, we can significantly minimize the accumulation of interest costs and avoid resorting to excessive debt in such situations. The cost of incurring debt is primarily attributed to the accruing interest, resulting in a final repayment amount that exceeds the initially borrowed sum. This stems from the imposition of a percentage-based charge, effectively elevating the total payment to approximately $6,500, rather than limited to the original $5,000. If you intend to acquire a credit card or loan, it is crucial to consider a few pieces of information. Prior to obtaining a credit card, it is crucial to ensure your ability to settle the outstanding balance on a monthly basis. Determine the prevailing interest rate and establish notifications to ensure prompt payment of the monthly outstanding balance.

In relation to the subject of debt, it is advisable to refrain from incurring debt in order to meet your daily expenses. This will solely lead you into an increasingly dire situation on a month-to-month basis. Your expenditures are advised to constitute no more than 80% of your earnings. If one's current lifestyle exceeds their financial means, they will inevitably incur debt. Moreover, any unforeseen circumstances such as job loss or financial crises would leave no margin for error. Which, realistically speaking, can occur at any given time, making it crucial to be adequately prepared rather than caught off guard. Ensure your own well-being and adhere to a lifestyle that promotes financial prudence. Your monthly earnings must be adequate to sustain a respectable standard of living while also enabling you to set aside funds on a regular basis.

Bathrooms

When implementing minimalistic principles throughout their homes, individuals frequently overlook the bathroom, allowing it to become a repository for an abundance of discarded, worn-out, and insignificant possessions. During the process of curating a minimalist environment within your home, it is advisable to allocate particular focus to your bathroom area. It is recommended to promptly discard and remove any residual toothpaste tubes, empty shampoo containers, air fresheners, breath fresheners, remaining soap remnants, and used razors that are occupying unnecessary storage space within your bathroom cabinet. If there are any items of which you have duplicates, kindly discard them accordingly. If you possess a pair of hairbrushes and exclusively utilize one, discard the additional brush.

Frequently, we obtain and preserve items in advance, intending to utilize them at a later point. However, more often than not, these possessions decay and go untouched, never fulfilling their intended purpose for us. If one possesses an extensive assortment of perfumes or body sprays, upon close examination, it is highly likely that numerous scarcely used bottles, occupying a significant amount of space on a surface, would be discovered to be merely half-filled. This behavior is a result of quickly acquiring new and intriguing items, only to subsequently neglect those possessions already in one's possession with the intention of using them at a later moment, which often proves to be illusory.

Your bathroom should exclusively consist of essential items. The presence of vacant cartons, utilized toilet paper rolls, and an abundance of towels is unnecessary. It is essential to ensure that an adequate quantity of towels, tissue paper rolls, scrubs, sponges, and similar items are present, as per the necessary requirements. If you proactively acquire additional items in advance, and if such an approach enhances the quality of your life, store these items in your designated storeroom or consider installing a compact storage cabinet within your bathroom, should there exist sufficient space for such a provision.

Certain individuals enjoy enhancing the aesthetic appeal of their bathrooms by incorporating pleasant pictures, wall art, and botanical elements. If that is your inclination and engaging in such activities brings you joy, I wholeheartedly encourage you to pursue them. Nevertheless, in the event that supplementary or embellishing elements are incorporated into your bathroom, it is important to bear in mind the necessity of frequent cleaning. The concept of minimalism fosters cleanliness, as it contributes to a sense of tranquility. Consequently, if objects hold genuine significance for you, they may be incorporated into your minimalistic lifestyle, provided they are appropriately maintained.

Living Area/ Lounge

If your residence includes a living room or lounge, it is advisable to tidy up the space, taking into consideration its dimensions and intended function. Sufficient seating must be provided to accommodate all household members and occasional guests, particularly if visitors are frequent. Nevertheless, if the population of individuals residing in your household is limited to 2 or 3, and the occurrence of visitors is infrequent, it becomes superfluous to possess seating arrangements capable of accommodating 12 individuals. One or two sofas, accompanied by a corresponding number of chairs, will effectively serve the purpose.

There exist various forms of minimalism, with 'American Minimalism' and 'Japanese Minimalism' representing two overarching categories. American minimalism promotes the retention of items that hold genuine significance and contribute value to one's life. Conversely, Japanese minimalism advocates for the deliberate elimination of possessions that are considered nonessential, challenging assumed needs rooted in personal beliefs. If one is convinced of the necessity of a couch, it will be retained; alternatively, if one is aware of the consistently available option to sit upon the floor, the couch will be relinquished as well.

If one desires to maintain a lifestyle of utmost simplicity, eliminating all but the most essential possessions and furnishings, one may adopt the principles of Japanese minimalism. According to this philosophy, traditional dining tables and couches are deemed unnecessary, as individuals can comfortably sit upon cushions on the floor and partake in meals at tables furnished with small stools or even directly on the floor. Considering the greater stringency and demand for rigorous discipline in the Japanese variant of minimalism, it is recommended to commence with the American variant and gradually transition towards the Japanese approach.

Certain individuals also derive pleasure from retaining vases, ornaments, and cherished mementos from their formative years and bygone days, which serve as poignant reminders of treasured memories within the confines of their living quarters. If you possess an exceptionally memorable keepsake, such as a medal commemorating your first victorious debate or a petite mosaic ornament obtained during a remarkable vacation to Turkey in the company of your family, and you harbor a desire to retain it, kindly exercise that right. Nevertheless, if you find that your living room is cluttered with numerous items that are neglected, covered in dust, and no longer hold any sentimental value, it would be wise to carefully examine and organize your possessions, discarding excess items and only retaining a select few.

Define Yourself

If one were to inquire about the concept of deriving pleasure from life, it is likely that the responses received would encompass the possession of a spacious residence, the indulgence of driving high-end automobiles, or the adornment of designer attire.

And thus, this serves as the underlying cause for the majority of our issues. As our attention becomes increasingly fixated on amassing wealth or achieving success, there is a heightened likelihood of relinquishing our hold on the things that hold the highest significance.

One significant drawback associated with money. In the absence of it, we apprehend that our existence will be fraught with suffering. Once we ultimately grasp the concept, a desire for further knowledge emerges within us. It is rather intriguing how our living standards tend to elevate as a result of receiving a salary increase, thereby inadvertently intensifying our desires and ambitions.

However, it must be acknowledged that we can shoulder fifty percent of the responsibility for this mindset. The remaining fifty percent can be attributed to the state of our current global circumstances. On a daily basis, we are inundated with advertisements purporting that the acquisition of a new computer will enhance our efficiency or that a larger residence is optimal for familial welfare.

Consequently, each subsequent paycheck procures either duplicates of items we already possess or items that we have no intention of utilizing.

Additionally, there is the matter of striving to make a favorable impression on our acquaintances. Many of us are culpable of making purchases solely because a peer possesses the same item. We engage in this behavior as a means to satisfy our need for self-validation, ensuring that we are not surpassed by others.

However, amidst our pursuit of acquiring possessions, we often overlook the need to part with the belongings we currently possess. Over time, a significant amount of clutter gradually accumulates.

As we prioritize the pursuit of wealth, we squander valuable time and expend energy that could have been allocated towards our passions and interests. However, what we often overlook are the significant aspects of life.

What\\\'s Important in Life?

The responses to this inquiry shall differ contingent upon the individual consulted. However, it should be noted that amidst all the accurate responses, there will invariably exist a fundamental commonality - the factor of experience. And that is the sole paramount concern in one's existence.

When a purchase is made, its value tends to depreciate within a short span of a few days or weeks. As such, a desire for something different begins to emerge. However, once an experience is acquired, it becomes cherished.

A sojourn to a foreign land is always imbued with indelible memories. A journey embarked upon with cherished companions across the vast expanse of the nation remains etched in one's memory indefinitely. Rescuing your friend from a life-threatening situation is an accomplishment that you will proudly recount for years to come.

However, you will never derive satisfaction from boasting about the expanse of your residence or the magnitude of your earnings.

Reestablishing a Connection with Core Values

Embracing a minimalist lifestyle entails a transformation of one's mindset. If your mind is not inclined, no level of coercion will succeed in compelling you to declutter.

Allow me to outline the process of preparing your mind:

Recognize your core principles - each of us holds personal motives behind our actions. However, existence occasionally leads us to overlook the aspects we hold in highest regard. Commence by ascertaining your core principles. Do you find fulfillment in attending to the needs of others? Alternatively, "Or do you simply possess a deep appreciation for your own identity?"

Compose a written record of your principles onto a sheet of paper and audibly articulate them. You are required to retain this document and peruse its contents nightly before retiring for the evening. Your actions ought to be guided by your underlying principles.

The "Why" Examination - on a sheet of paper, record the activities or responsibilities that have been occupying your time recently.

For instance, if you have been engaged in part-time employment, reflect upon the rationale behind such a decision. Are you endeavoring to make a purchase of a new automobile? Are you endeavoring to leave a lasting impression on someone? Should your responses fail to align with your core principles, thereby deviating from your set priorities, it indicates a misdirected emphasis.

The "Mortality Examination" - envision yourself deceased. Consider a scenario in which a person you hold dear inquires about your accomplishments of which you feel a sense of pride.

Please make a record of your responses. Are these the matters upon which you are presently directing your attention, or are they not? If that is not the case, then it is advisable to thoroughly reconsider and reassess the trajectory of your life.

Allocate resources to areas of focus

The key objective of minimalism does not revolve primarily around the preservation of time, money, and energy. Instead, the lifestyle acts as a vehicle for allocating the necessary resources towards what one deems as their foremost priorities.

Priorities can be described as the elements that greatly utilize your resources. Occasionally, however, the priorities you articulate may not align with the ones that consume the majority of your time and energy. As an illustration, it is incongruous to claim that one's work is of utmost importance while consistently engaging in socializing and traveling for leisure purposes. If you are unable to allocate even a brief moment to converse with your child, spouse, and/or parents, it would be inaccurate to claim that it is your family.

The state of bewilderment is partially accentuated by the various disturbances in your surroundings. For example, there are those who mistakenly interpret the act of cleaning as an indication of productivity. It is more advantageous than disregarding disorder in any case. Nevertheless, the optimal scenario entails having minimal cleaning responsibilities, thus enabling you to devote greater attention to your primary occupational duties.

An additional illustration is the acquisition of a multitude of inexpensive merchandise during promotional events. It appears as though you have accumulated substantial savings. Indeed, the act of refraining from incurring unexpected expenditures is paramount in order to amass savings during sales events. If ensuring one's financial stability is a matter of importance, it is imperative to bear in mind this particular point.

If you happen to be a parent, it should be noted that purchasing excessively expensive toys and indulgent treats does not guarantee that your child will comprehend the reasons behind your diligent efforts. If you hold your child's well-being as paramount, it is imperative that you allocate quality time to them. Time is invaluable, unlike any tangible possessions.

Live Happier

Minimalism offers numerous benefits that contribute to a life filled with happiness. Carving out opportunities to foster strong relationships with loved ones and experiencing a greater sense of autonomy are among those benefits. By adopting minimalist habits to alleviate your debt, you are likely to experience an augmented sense of contentment as well. An alternative approach pertains to the elimination of elements that evoke sorrow.

Encountering your collection of memorabilia has the potential to elicit profound sentiments. Nevertheless, such emotions do not consistently exhibit positivity. If the purpose of that keepsake is to serve as a reminder of a joyous occasion, there is a possibility that you might inadvertently find yourself nostalgic for that particular moment. Retaining the mementos that evoke memories of your hardships and ultimate triumph will elicit a sense of gratitude for the latter. However, there exists within you a sense of melancholy associated with the endurance of difficulties.

Rather than physical souvenirs, the principles of minimalism advocate for the digitization of keepsakes. In this manner, the emotional bond to those possessions as well as the recollections they evoke will not be excessively potent. Furthermore, you will have greater autonomy in determining the times when it is necessary to recollect both the positive and negative moments, as your tendency to peruse photographs will be reduced. If those cherished keepsakes are elegantly showcased on the wall, a mere inadvertent glance in their direction could evoke a flood of nostalgic recollections. By lacking those immediate prompts, you are more likely to embrace the present moment.

It is imperative to bear in mind the importance of embracing the present and refraining from fixating on the future. You possess limited authority over the events of the present day, regardless. Initiate the utilization of such control by engaging in the act of decluttering, as recommended in the subsequent.

The Value Of Clearing Mental Clutter To Improve Your Life

As elucidated in the preceding , the deleterious repercussions of clutter encompass diversion, anxiety, and succumbing to immediate indulgence. As our level of stress increases, the likelihood of experiencing anxiety and engaging in excessive rumination also rises. In order to mitigate these vexing and occasionally perilous adverse effects, it is imperative that we engage in the process of decluttering our minds.

Engaging in the process of mental decluttering can prove to be quite challenging. It necessitates substantial effort and potentially entails making challenging decisions. At times, you will be required to opt for the arduous route rather than the convenient one. However, upon becoming aware of the advantages that await one upon eliminating clutter from one's life, it becomes significantly more effortless to opt for the correct decision.

Mental clutter hampers your progress in every aspect. Provided that your lifestyle remains disorganized, characterized by a plethora of activities and responsibilities that do not align with your objectives, you will encounter adverse consequences. The pursuit of success, defined individually, becomes arduous when one's time is consumed within a disordered dwelling or workspace, grappling with an unsettled state of mind. To eliminate mental clutter entails minimizing the influence of these adverse consequences and, ultimately, eradicating their grasp over you entirely. Engaging in the process of decluttering enables you to address the underlying issue at its core. You actively minimize the elements in your life that add to stress and refrain from resorting to impulsive acquisitions as a means to regulate your emotions. By doing this, you are able to allocate more time that you would have otherwise expended on either carrying out insignificant tasks or being preoccupied with these stress inducers. Streamlining your thought processes allows for greater allocation of time towards relaxation, resulting in substantial enhancements to one's mental well-being. These are desirable outcomes that justify and merit the exertion of any degree of effort necessary to attain them.

The Role of Mind Decluttering in Facilitating Ongoing Personal Development

If one has experienced the act of spring cleaning, they can attest to the transformative experience of turning a disarray of antiquated belongings, heaps of garments, and miscellaneous clutter into an orderly and organized living space. The job can be somewhat fatiguing, and it is likely to provide you with a beneficial physical exercise. One might dedicate a full day to discarding items and reorganizing the remaining belongings, or alternatively, opt to divide the task into several days or weeks for its completion. Regardless of the approach you take, a feeling of fulfillment arises from successfully completing a task. Upon observing one's surroundings and perceiving everything neatly arranged, devoid of any items that have remained stagnant and unused, a sense of satisfaction arises with regard to one's achievements. It is akin to affording oneself the prospect of commencing anew, and so long as one ensures minimal accumulation and refrains from unnecessary purchases, the need to repeat the procedure in the forthcoming spring season shall be obviated.

As mental decluttering adheres to the same principles as minimalist interior design, it can yield comparable outcomes. By eliminating mental clutter, we grant ourselves a heightened sense of liberation. Our schedules become more flexible, our minds become unencumbered by distractions, and the incessant background noise of our thoughts is tranquilized. In the absence of cognitive distractions, we are able to experience a profound sense of inner tranquility that has eluded us for an extended period of time. In addition to all these advantages, we also facilitate a shift in our focus towards the future instead of dwelling on the past. As we commence contemplating our future course, we can initiate the process of relinquishing any obligations that do not contribute to the attainment of our objectives, thereby enhancing our efficiency and promoting a sense of calmness simultaneously.

The Fallacy of Self-Esteem Derived from Social Standing

This associated work of fiction can be deemed relatively straightforward. Your inherent worth as an individual does not reside in any intrinsic aspect of your being. It does not encompass your aspirations, desires, aspirations, inclinations, affections, or individual enigma.

It does not come to you naturally. Alternatively, it is bestowed by individuals. If individuals acknowledge and affirm your existence and identity, then you hold a rightful place as a significant individual. If one asserts that you are merely an anonymous presence among the masses, then that becomes your predetermined destiny. Your responsibility, therefore, is to exert diligent effort akin to that of a canine in order to attain the desired societal standing.

It is imperative to maintain pace with one's neighbors. If one observes their arrival in a Mercedes vehicle to a freshly built garage, it is necessary for one to enter their own newly constructed garage in possession of a brand-new Mercedes. In the event that, two years henceforth, they are observed arriving in a BMW, it shall be incumbent upon you to emulate their choice of vehicle.

The concept revolves around one's social standing, which pertains to how one is perceived by others. If one is perceived as significant or important, then they are considered to hold such status. Whether or not you perceive yourself as someone of significance holds little relevance, given that nobody is giving any attention.

According to this work of fiction, there is a lack of concern or interest from others. Rather, the focus is primarily on outward manifestations of one's social standing. If you belong to the middle class, it would be advisable for you to own a vehicle that is befitting of your socioeconomic status. If you belong to the upper socioeconomic group, it is advisable to possess a vehicle that aligns with this status, reside in a distinguished neighborhood, and adorn oneself with attire and accessories befitting of the upper echelons of society. This is because, ultimately, one's standing is determined by the way they are perceived by others, which is influenced by factors such as attire, place of residence, educational background, social circle, and affiliations.

When all these factors are taken into account, individuals form specific perceptions. These impressions are what determine your value. One can vociferate atop the tallest peak to proclaim their identity, yet they would find the efforts fruitless in the eyes of the institutional arrangement, as lacking the outward symbols of substantial societal standing, or rather, a consequential standing.

The Fallacy of the Pseudo-Progressive Mentality

This work of fiction possesses a myriad of diverse iterations. Alternate formulations in a formal tone could include: - This adage can also be expressed as "increasing quantity corresponds to increasing quality," "greater size implies greater quality," "novelty is indicative of superiority," or "superiority is directly proportional to height." Nonetheless, a shared aspect among all of them is the notion of "improvement."

It is a conceptual notion that organizes one's life in a chronological or graphical representation. The greater one's accumulation of assets and possessions, both in terms of financial worth and physical size, the more advantageous one's circumstances become. This raises the question: What truly defines the term "superior"? Based on this line of thought, it possesses a quantitative nature.

An individual possessing a net worth of $100,000 is in a more advantageous financial position compared to someone with a net worth of $10,000. An individual with a net worth of $10,000,000 surpasses someone with a net worth of $100,000. This perspective fails to acknowledge the inherent worth of labor or its significance within society. It inherently fails to consider the positive impact you create in the lives of individuals. It possesses a fundamental metric. One is either engaged in substantial monetary gain and possesses considerable net worth, or one is not.

The underlying concept entails that a higher monetary value attributed to one's work signifies its genuine worth. It is readily apparent how this line of reasoning crumbles, yet a multitude of individuals who subscribe to this fallacy express no regard for the incongruity. They display an utter lack of concern regarding the notable disparity that exists between the price and the inherent value associated with any given object.

It is possible that you are under the assumption that air is without cost, however, allow me to inform you that if one were to abruptly obstruct your access to oxygen at this precise moment, you would swiftly realize the immense value associated with it. The aforementioned principle is equally applicable to the matters that we perceive as highly significant and of great worth. Ultimately, as previously stated in the introduction, it is highly unlikely that an individual in their final moments of life would express a desire to have dedicated more time towards working excessive hours beyond their regular duties. I desire to acquire an increased quantity of items. I desire to make a stronger positive impression on a greater number of individuals.

www.ingramcontent.com/pod-product-compliance
Lightning Source LLC
Chambersburg PA
CBHW052145110526
44591CB00012B/1864